Arabic for Archaeologists

Cover: The early 6th century pre-Islamic Arabic inscription from Umm al-Jimal

ISBN: 978-9957-8543-4-8

Published by: ACOR, Amman, Jordan
Design and layout: Isabelle Ruben
Printed by: National Press, Amman, Jordan

المملكة الأردنية الهاشمية
رقم الايداع لدى دائرة
المكتبة الوطنية
٢٠٠٩\٥\١٨٧٣

Author: Schick, Robert
Arabic for Archaeologists
Amman: American Center of Oriental Research, 2009
(36)p.
Deposit No.: 2009/5/1873

Preface

In 1963, Paul W. Lapp published the first edition of *Arabic for the Beginner in Archaeology* with Najua Husseini. At that time he was Director of the Jerusalem School of the American Schools of Oriental Research where during 1965-68 he served as the Professor of Archaeology. In the 1960s he conducted excavations at many sites, including Iraq al-Amir, Tell er-Rumeith and Bab edh-Dhra'. His death in 1970 on Cyprus due to an accident ended an active career and vital life. His widow, Nancy L. Lapp, has continued the work of publishing his excavation material.

Nancy Lapp produced in 1971 a revised edition of this booklet as amended by Bishara Zoughbi, and she kept this pocket-sized publication in circulation for more than 35 years (see original prefaces that follow). In spring 2008 when she was a fellow at ACOR, she decided it was the time to turn over the publication to ACOR. As she chaired ACOR's fellowship committee for eighteen years, she has offered this book for future generations of young archaeologists and has committed the proceeds to the endowment of the ACOR Library.

Robert Schick was in Amman on a fellowship at ACOR when the change of publisher was discussed. He offered to work on this new version, which has taken new shape in form and content but maintains the spirit of the original creation. His field experience in Jordan since 1980 has involved many sites. He is eminently suited to be responsible for this new edition given his understanding of dig life, his fluency in Arabic, and his expertise as a scholar of the Late Antique and Islamic periods in the region.

A tie between the first edition and this current one is Mohammed Adawi, known as Abu Ahmed to the countless number of visitors to ACOR who have enjoyed his meals since its inception in 1968. He started working for the school in Jerusalem in 1960, and when he was consulted for some terms in spring 2008, he noted he had also assisted Paul Lapp those many years ago.

When in the field, you will surely hear different words and phrases than those provided here. You may want to annotate your copy with these colloquial variants. We hope this book will benefit many excavation team members in the years to come.

Barbara A. Porter
ACOR Director
Amman, 2009

Preface to the Fourth Printing
Revised

The first edition of this little book was compiled twenty-seven years ago by my late husband, Paul W. Lapp, and Najua Husseini. In 1971 I had it reprinted with corrections and additions. Bishara Zoughbi of Bethlehem who had worked several years in field archaeology with Paul as a surveyor and draftsman assisted with this edition. It had to be reprinted in 1981 and is now out-of-print again.

With this edition many corrections have been made in the transliterations, and the text has been completely re-set. Again, we offer it as a tribute to Paul, twenty years after his death, in hope that those who come to Palestine and Jordan to supervise archaeological field work, as he expressed in 1963, "will find it helpful in learning to communicate in an effective and friendly manner with their laborers as rapidly as possible."

April 26, 1990
Nancy L. Lapp

Preface to the First Edition

ARABIC FOR THE BEGINNER IN ARCHAEOLOGY

This little pocketbook contains some two hundred words and phrases with colloquial Jerusalem Arabic and partly village Arabic equivalents in transcription and Arabic characters. The selection has no scientific basis. Those words which have become familiar and proved most useful to one archaeologist in the last few years are grouped in several categories, and English words are listed alphabetically with their equivalents at the end. The lists have been prepared by one who makes no claim to be a specialist, or even conversant, in Arabic.

I am indebted to Miss Najua Husseini of the Jordan Department of Antiquities for preparing the Arabic equivalents, to Professor Wm. F. Stinespring for detailed corrections of the transcriptions, and to Miss Beatrice Habesh of the Commercial Press for technical advice in getting the booklet into print. It is offered with the hope that those who come to Jordan to supervise archaeological field work for the first time will find it helpful in learning to communicate in an effective and friendly manner with their laborers as rapidly as possible.

June 10, 1963
Paul W. Lapp

Basic Grammar

Arabic does not use an indefinite article "a". The definite article "the" is "al-". For ease of pronunciation, the "l", however often assimilates to the first letter of the following noun: "mawqi'" (an archaeological site) "al-mawqi'" (the archaeological site); "shanta" (a backpack) "ash-shanta" (the backpack).

Masculine nouns and adjectives are made feminine by adding an "a" at the end: "mudīr" (director – masculine) – "mudīra" (director – feminine), "tālib" (student – masculine) – "tāliba" (student – feminine).

Plurals of feminine nouns are normally made by replacing the "a" with an "āt" at the end of the word: "'arabāya" (wheelbarrow) – "'arabāyāt" (wheel-barrows). Plurals of masculine nouns have many forms so have to be learned individually; only a few are listed.

Adjectives follow nouns: "shughl mumtāz" (excellent work) "ar-rujm al-kebīr" (the large rock pile), "adh-dhahab at-turkī" (the Turkish gold), "al-ma'bad an-nabatī" (the Nabatean temple).

Adjectives can sometimes be formed from nouns by adding an "ī" at the end: "dhahab" (gold) "dhahabī" (golden), "ḥadīd" (iron) "al-'asr al-ḥadīdī" (the Iron Age).

When a noun is followed by an attached pronoun or possessive noun, the definite article is not used: "aj-jihāz" (the gadget) "jihāzu" (his gadget) "jihāz al-mashrū'" (the project's gadget).

The “a” at the end of feminine singular nouns changes to “at” when followed by an attached pronoun or possessive noun: “Wein ash-shanta” (Where is the backpack?) – “Wein shantatī” (Where is my backpack?), “al-mudīra” (the director) “mudīrathum” (their director) “mudīrat al-ma‘had” (the institute director).

Arabic does not use a verb “to be” in the present tense: “sawwāq al-‘arabāya majnūn” (the wheelbarrow driver is crazy). “kān” is used in the past tense: “sawwāq al-‘arabaya kān majnūn” (the wheelbarrow driver was crazy).

Imperative verbs are formed from the verb stem for masculine singular. Feminine singular adds an “i” at the end, and plural adds an “u” at the end:
“iḥfir” (Dig! masculine singular) احفر
“iḥfirī” (Dig! feminine singular) احفري
“iḥfirū” (Dig! plural) احفرو

Negative imperatives are formed by adding the prefix “mat”: “matiḥfir hōn” (Don’t dig here) ماتحفر هون

In the following pages, occasional example phrases are given in italics. The transliteration of the Arabic is simplified; diacritical dots are used only with the hard Arabic “ḥ” needed to clearly distinguish “th” and “sh” as in the English words “the” and “she” from “tḥ” and “sḥ” pronounced as two separate letters.

The Arabic letter “ق” is transliterated here as “q”, although it is often pronounced “g” or is silent. The vowel “a” can blend into “e” or “i” in colloquial pronunciation.

Present tense verbs begin with the letter "b" as a prefix:

bā-	I	I bring	bajīb	بجيب
bin-	We	we bring	binjīb	بنجيب
bit-	You (m. sing.)	you bring	bitjīb	بتجيب
bit-ī	You (f. sing.)	you bring	bitjībī	بتجيبي
bit-ū	You (pl.)	you bring	bitjībū	بنجيبو
biy-	He	he brings	biyjīb	بيجيب
bit-	She	she brings	bitjīb	بتجيب
biy-ū	They	they bring	biyjībū	بيجيبو

The conjugation for "want" is different:

I want	biddī	بدي
We want	biddnā	بدنا
You (m. sing.)	biddak	بدك
You (f. sing.)	biddik	بدك
You (pl.)	biddku	بدكو
He wants	bidduh	بده
She wants	biddhā	بدها
They want	biddhum	بدهم

Particles/Prepositions

Inside	juwwā	جوا
Outside	barrā	برا
In	fī	في
On	'alā	على
To	ilā	الى
From	min	من
Yes	aywa/na'am	ايوه/نعم
No	lā	لا
There is	fī	في
There is not	māfī/māfīsh/fīsh	
(All three variants are in common use)		مافي/مافيش/فش
I, you, etc. have no brains	*māfī mukh*	مافي مخ
There was not	makān fī	ماكان في
There was no pottery in the bucket	*makān fī fukhār fī ad-dalu*	ماكان في فخار في الدلو
Why?	leish/liweish	ليش/لويش
Where?	wein?	وين
Here	hōn	هون
Why am I here?	*leish anā hōn*	ليش انا هون
There	hinākَ	هناك

Pronouns

This	hādha	هذا
What	shū/esh	شو/ايش
Who?	mīn?	مين

I	anā	انا
We	eḥnā/niḥnā	نحنا/ احنا
You (m. sing.)	inta	انت
You (f. sing.)	intī	انتي
You (pl.)	intū	انتو
He	huwa	هوه
She	hiya	هي
They	humma/humm	همه/هم

Pronouns attached to the end of a preceeding noun:

My	-ī	aghradī (my stuff) اغراضي
Our	-nā	aghradnā (our stuff) اغراضنا
Your (m. sing.)	-ak	aghradak (your stuff) اغراضك
Your (f. sing.)	-ik	aghradik (your stuff) اغراضك
Your (pl.)	-ku	aghradku (your stuff) اغراضكو
His	-u	aghradu (his stuff) اغراضه
Her	-hā	aghradhā (her stuff) اغراضها
Their	-hum	aghradhum (their stuff) اغراضهم

General Archaeological Terms

Antiquities	āthār	آثار
Science	‘ilm	علم
Archaeology	‘ilm al-āthār	علم الآثار
Archaeological	atharī	اثري
Heritage	turāth	تراث
History	tārīkh	تاريخ
Anthropology	‘ilm al-insān	علم الانسان
Geology	jiyulūjiyā	جيولوجيا
Archaeological site	mawqī‘ atharī	موقع أثري
Project	mashrū‘	مشروع
Mission	bi‘tha	بعثة
Excavation	ḥafriya, pl. ḥafrīyāt	حفرية حفريات
Excavation project	mashrū‘ al-ḥafrīya	مشروع الحفريه
Survey	masḥ/ masḥ atharī	مسح / مسح أثري
Restoration	tarmīm	ترميم
Restoration project	mashrū‘ tarmīm	مشروع ترميم
Storeroom	mustawda‘/ makhzan	مستودع / مخزن
Museum	matḥaf	متحف

Laboratory	mukhtabar	مختبر
Office	maktab	مكتب
School	madrasa	مدرسة
Institute	ma'had	معهد
British Institute	al-ma'had al-brītānī	المعهد البريطاني
French Institute	al-ma'had al-faransī	المعهد الفرنسي
German Institute	al-ma'had al-almānī	المعهد الالماني
ACOR	al-markaz al-amrīkī lil-abḥāth ash-sharqīya	المركز الامريكي للابحاث الشرقية
Department	dā'ira	دائرة
Department of Antiquities	dā'irat al-āthār	دائرة الآثار

Personnel

Expert	khabīr	خبير
Archaeologist	khabīr āthār	خبير آثار
Director	mudīr	مدير
Assistant	musā'id	مساعد
Assistant director	musā'id mudīr	مساعد مدير

District inspector	mufattish	مفتش
Department representative	mandūb	مندوب
Person in charge	mas'ūl	مسؤول
Who is in charge?	*mīn al-mas'ūl?*	مين المسؤول
Camp manager	mudabbir	مدبر
Supervisor	mushrif	مشرف
Foreman	ma'allim	معلم
Worker	'āmil, pl. 'ummāl	عامل/ عمال
Driver	sawwāq/sāyiq	سواق/سايق
Wheelbarrow driver	sawwāq al-'arabaya	سواق العرباي
Guard	ḥāris	حارس
Cook	tabbākh	طباخ
Assistant cook	musā'id tabbākh	مساعد طباخ
Draftsman	rassām	رسام
Photographer	musāwwir	مصور
Architect/Engineer	muhandis	مهندس
Surveyor	massāḥ	مساح
Specialist in	mukhtass bi-	مختص ب
Bone specialist	*mukhtass bil-'adhām*	مختص بالعظام

Professor	ustāz	استاذ
Student	tālib	طالب
Conservator	murammim	مرمم
Museum curator	amīn mathaf	امين متحف
Landowner	sāḥib al-'ard	صاحب الارض
Thief	liss/ḥarāmī	لص/حرامي

Geological Terms

Dirt/Soil	turāb	تراب
Clay	tīn	طين
Sand	raml	رمل
Pebble	ḥiswa, pl. ḥasa	حصوه/ حصى
Cobble	dimis	دمس
Rock/Stone	ḥajar, pl. ḥijāra	حجر/حجارة
Boulder	sakhra	صخرة
Bedrock	sakhr	صخر
Ground	ard	ارض
Surface of the ground	satḥ al-ard	سطح الارض
Valley	wādī	وادي
Mountain	jabal	جبل

Plants

Plants	nabātāt	نباتات
Roots	judhūr	جذور
Seeds	bidhūr	بذور
Thorns	shōk	شوك
Tree	shajara, pl. ashjār	شجرة/اشجار
Underbrush/weeds	‘ushub	عشب

Animals

Animal	ḥaywān	حيوان
Camel	jamal	جمل
Donkey	ḥimār	حمار
Sheep/Goat	ghanam	غنم
Dog	kalb	كلب
Cat	bissa	بسة
Bird	‘asfūr	عصفور
Snake	ḥayya	حية
Scorpion	‘aqrab	عقرب
Cockroach	sarsūr	صرصور
Flies	dhubbān	ذبان
Mosquito	nāmūs	ناموس

Excavation and Architectural Terms

There is no good colloquial word for "locus;" "wiḥda athārīya" (archaeological unit), "wiḥdat ḥafr" (excavation unit), or "zāhira" (phenomenon) are artifical neologisms that workmen will not understand: You might as well just say "locus" لوكاس.

Unit	wiḥda	وحدة
Layer	tabaqa	طبقة
Empty space	farāgh	فراغ
Foundation	asās	اساس
Side	janb	جنب
Pit	jōra	جورة
Balk	qāti'	قاطع
Balk section	maqta'	مقطع
Excavation area	muntiqat ḥafr	منطقة حفر
Excavation trench	khandaq	خندق
Excavation square	murabba'	مربعة
Excavation dump	tamam	طمم
Ruin	khirba	خربة
Tell	tall/tell	تل
Archaeological remains	baqāyā athariya	بقايا اثرية
Pile of dirt	turāba	ترابة

Pile of rocks	rujm	رجم
Room	ghurfa	غرفة
Door	bāb	باب
Roof	saqif	سقف
Floor/Surface	ardīya	ارضية
Arch	qōs	قوس
Wall	ḥeit/jidār	حيط/جدار
City wall	sūr	سور
Building	mabna	مبنى
House	beit/dār	بيت/دار
Large building/ Palace	qasr	قصر
Fortess/Citadel	qal'a	قلعة
Temple	ma'bad	معبد
Courtyard	ḥōsh	حوش
Street/Road/Path	tarīq	طريق
Water channel	qanāt mayya	قناة ميه
Cave	maghāra	مغارة
Press	ma'sara	معصرة
Olive oil press	ma'sarat zeit	معصرة زيت
Wine press	ma'sarat 'ināb	معصرة عنب
Bread oven	tabūn/tannūr	طابون/تنور

Oven/Kiln	furn	فرن
Grave/Tomb	qabr, pl. qubūr	قبر/قبور
Cemetery	maqbara	مقبرة
Tower	burj	برج
Military encampment	mu‘askar	معسكر
Mosque	masjid	مسجد
Church	kanīsa	كنيسة
Quarry	maḥjar	محجر
Cistern	bīr	بير
Reservoir	birka	بركة

Artifacts

Piece	qit‘a	قطعة
Part	juz‘	جزء
Sample	‘ayyina	عينة
Pottery	fukhār	فخار
Sherd	shiqfa, pl. shuqaf/ qit‘a	شقفة/ شقف قطعة
Pottery sherds	shuqaf fukhār	شقف فخار
Jar	jārra	جرة

Large water jar	zīr	زير
Jug	ibrīq	ابريق
Bowl	saḥn	صحن
Lamp	sirāj	سراج
Seal/Stamp	khitim	ختم
Statue	timthāl	تمثال
Figurine	timthāl saghīr	تمثال صغير
Glass	qazaz	قزاز
Flint	suwwān	صوان
Tool	adāh, pl. adawāt	اداة/ادوات
Stone tools	adawāt ḥajarīya	ادوات حجرية
Bone	'adhm, pl. 'adhām	عظم/عظام
Iron	ḥadīd	حديد
Bronze	bronz	برونز
Silver	fidda	فضة
Gold	dhahab	ذهب
Coin	'imla	عملة
Shell	sadaf	صدف
Writing	kitāba	كتابة
Mosaic	fusayfisā'	فسيفساء
Marble	rukhām	رخام

Wood	khashab	خشب
Garbage	zabāla/izbāla	زبالة
Ash	sakan/ramād	سكن/رماد
Charcoal	faḥm	فحم
Plaster	qisāra/iqsara	قصارة
Brick	tūba, pl. tūb	طوبه/طوب
Column	‘amūd	عمود
Paving stone	balāta	بلاطة

Colors

Color	lōn	لون
Black	aswad	اسود
Blue	azraq	ازرق
Brown	bunnī	بني
Green	akhdar	اخضر
Grey	ramādī	رمادي
Red	aḥmar	احمر
Yellow	asfar	اصفر
White	abyad	ابيض
Light	fātiḥ	فاتح
Dark	ghāmiq	غامق

Equipment

Anything/ Something	ishī	اشـي
Is there anything in the storeroom?	*fī ishī fil-mustawda'?*	فـي اشـي فـي المسـتودع
Stuff	aghrād	اغراض
Tools/Equipment	'idda	عـدة
Gadget/Instrument	jihāz	جـهاز
Electronic device	jihāz elektronī	جـهاز الـكـتروني
Computer	ḥasūb/ kombyuter	حـاسـوب/ كـمبيوتر
Plastic bag	kīs, pl. akyās/ kīs blāstīk	كـيس, اكـياس/ كـيس بلاسـتيك
Paper bag	kīs waraq	كـيس ورق
Shoulder bag/ Backpack	shanta	شـنطة
Envelope	zarf	ظرف
Tag/Label	bitāqa	بطاقة
Bucket	dalu	دلو
Pen	qalam	قلم
Pencil	qalam rasās	قلم رصاص
Eraser	maḥāya	محاية
Notebook	daftar	دفتر
Ruler	mastara	مسـطرة

Piece of paper	waraqa, pl. awrāq	ورقة/اوراق
Piece of graph paper	waraqat rasm bayānī	ورقة رسم بياني
Sieve	munkhul	منخل
Plumb bob	bulbul	بلبل
Pick	fās	فاس
Hand pick	mankūsh/ minkāsh	منكوش/ منكاش
Trowel	mastarīn	مسطرين
Hoe	majrafa	مجرفة
Bulldozer	jarrāfa	جرافة
Rubber tire basket	quffa, pl. qufaf	قفة/قفف
Hammer	shākūsh	شاكوش
Sledge hammer	mhadda	مهدة
Dust pan	majrūd	مجرود
Saw	minshār	منشار
String	kheit	خيط
Rope	ḥabl	حبل
Nail	musmār	مسمار
Short meter tape	mitir	متر
Long meter tape	karkar	كركر
Brush	furshāya	فرشايه

Broom	muknisa	مكنسة
Wheelbarrow	‘arabāya	عرباية
Level	mīzān	ميزان
Ladder	sillam	سلم
Plan	mukhattat	مخطط
Report	taqrīr	تقرير

Adjectives

Few	qalīl	قليل
Many	kathir	كثير
Full	malyān	مليان
Empty	fādī	فاضي
Dirty	wasakh	وسخ
Clean	nadīf	نظيف
Broken	maksūr	مكسور
Excellent	mumtāz	ممتاز
Good	kwayis/mnīḥ	كويس/ منيح
Lost	dāyi‘	ضايع
North	shamāl	شمال
South	janūb	جنوب
East	sharq	شرق
West	gharb	غرب

Right	yamīn	يمين
Left	shmāl	شمال
Horizontal	ufuqī	افقي
Vertical	‘āmūdī	عامودي
Level	mustawī	مستوي
Smooth	nā‘im	ناعم
Rough	khashin	خشن
Crazy	majnūn	مجنون
Lazy	kaslān	كسلان
Industrious	nashīt	نشيط
Clever	shātir	شاطر

Imperative Verbs

Take	khudh	خذ
Take the pick	*khudh al-fās*	خذ الفاس
Work	ishtaghil	اشتغل
Work more	*ishtaghil akthar*	اشتغل اكثر
Dig	iḥfir	احفر
Dig here	*iḥfir hōn*	احفر هون
Give	‘atī	أعطي
Give me the trowel	*‘atīnī al-mastarīn*	أعطيني المسطرين

Fill	‘abī	عبي
Fill the guffa	*‘abī al-quffa*	عبي القفة
Carry/take away	shīl	شيل
Take the dirt away	*shīl al-turab*	شيل التراب
Dump	kib	كب
Dump the wheel-barrow on the excavation dump	*kib al-‘arabāya ‘ala at-tamam*	كب العرباية على الطمم
Drive	sūq	سوق
Drive the wheelbarrow	*sūq al-‘arabāya*	سوق العرباية
Lift	irfa‘	ارفع
Lift up the rocks	*irfa‘ al-ḥijāra*	ارفع الحجارة
Look for	dawwir ‘ala	دوّر على
Look out for the Turkish gold	*dawwir ‘ala adh-dhahab at-turki*	دوّر على الذهب التركي
Put	ḥutt	حط
Put the bucket over there	*ḥutt al-dalu hinak*	حط الدلو هناك
Bring	jīb	جيب
Bring the bag	*jīb al-kīs*	جيب الكيس
Sift	nakhkhil	نخل
Shift the dirt	*nakhkhil at-turāb*	نخل التراب
Come	ta‘āl	تعال

Come here	*ta'āl hōn*	تعال هون
Go	rūḥ	روح
Go over there	*rūḥ hinād*	روح هناك
Go in	fūt 'ala	فوت على
Go into the square	*fūt 'ala al-murabba'*	فوت على المربعة
Go out	itla'	اطلع
Go out of the square	*itla' min al-murabba'*	اطلع من المربعة
Organize/ Straighten up	zabbit	زبط
Straighten up the excavation dump	*zabbit at-tamam*	زبط الطمم
Organize/arrange	dabbir	دبّر
Get your act together	*dabbir ḥālak*	دبّر حالك
Gather up	limm	لم
Collect the tools	*limm al-'idda*	لم العدة
Be careful	dīr bālak/uw'a	دير بالك/اوعى
Watch out for the balk	*dīr bālak/uw'a min al-qāti'*	دير بالك/اوعى من القاطع
Leave it	khalī	خليه
Leave it in its place	*khalī fī makānu*	خليه في مكانه
Destroy	kharrib	خرب
Don't destroy the balk	*matkharrib al-qāti'*	ماتخرب القاطع

Other Verbs

Know	‘irif	عرف
I don’t know	*ana mish ‘ārif*	انا مش عارف
Understand	fihim	فهم
I don’t understand	*ana mish fāhim*	انا مش فاهم
Come on/Hurry up!	yālla	يلاَ
Hurry up, there’s no time	*yāllā, māfi waqt*	يلاَ مافي وقت

Adverbs

Slowly	bi-shwaysh/ shway shway	بشويش/ شوي شوي
Quickly	bi-sur‘a	بسرعة

Numbers

One	wāḥid	واحد
Two	ithnein/itnein	اثنين
Three	thalātha/talāta	ثلاثة
Four	arb‘a	اربعة
Five	khamsa	خمسة
Six	sitta	ستة
Seven	sab‘a	سبعة
Eight	thamānya	ثمانية

Nine	tis'a	تسعة
Ten	'ashara	عشرة
Twenty	'ishrīn	عشرين
One hundred	miyya	مِية
One thousand	alf	الف
First	awwal	اول
Second	thānī	ثاني

Time

Time	waqt/waqat	وقت
When?	emta/mata?	ايمتى/متى
Early	bakīr	بكّير
Late	mitakhir	متأخر
Morning	as-subuḥ	الصبح
Noon	ad-duhr	الظهر
Afternoon	al-'asr	العصر
Evening	al-masa	المساء
Night	al-leil	الليل
Breaktime	istirāḥa	استراحة
Minute	daqīqa	دقيقة
Hour	sā'a	ساعة
Day	yōm	يوم

Yesterday	imbāriḥ/ams	امبارح/امس
Day before yesterday	awwal imbāriḥ	اول امبارح
Tomorrow	bukra	بكره
Day after tomorrow	ba‘d bukra	بعد بكره
Week	usbū‘	اسبوع
Month	shahr	شهر
Season	mawsim	موسم
Year	sana/‘amm	سنة/عام
Century	qarin	قرن
Period	fatra	فترة
Age	‘asir	عصر
B.C./B.C.E.	qabl al-milād	قبل الميلاد
A.D./C.E.	mīlādī	ميلادي
Sunday	yom al-aḥad	يوم الاحد
Monday	yom al-ithnein	يوم الاثنين
Tuesday	yom ath-thalātha	يوم الثلاثاء
Wednesday	yom al-arb‘a	يوم الاربعاء
Thursday	yom al-khamīs	يوم الخميس
Friday	yom aj-jum‘a	يوم الجمعة
Saturday	yom as-sabt	يوم السبت

Holiday	‘īd	عيد
Day off	‘utla	عطلة

Food

Breakfast	futūr	فطور
Second breakfast	futūr thānī	فطور ثاني
Lunch	ghada	غداء
Supper	‘asha	عشاء
Water	may/mayya	مَيّة
Tea	shāy	شاي
Coffee	qahwa	قهوة
Fruit juice	‘asīr	عصير
Cup/Glass	kāsa	كاسة
Cup of tea	kāsat shāy	كاسة شاي
Sugar	sukkar	سكر
Salt	malḥ	ملح
Bread	khubiz	خبز
Fruit	fawākih	فواكه
Vegetables	khudār	خضار
Meat	laḥma	لحمة
Egg	beida	بيضة
Cheese	jibna	جبنة

Social Pleasantries

Hello	marḥaba	مرحبا
Hello (reply)	marḥabtein	مرحبتين
Peace be upon you	as-salām ‘alaykum	السلام عليكم
And upon you peace (reply)	wa-‘alaykum as-salām	وعليكم السلام
Goodbye	ma‘a as-salāma	مع السلامة
Good Morning	sabāḥ al-kheir	صباح الخير
Good Morning (reply)	sabāḥ an-nūr	صباح النور
Good Evening	masā al-kheir	مساء الخير
Good Evening (reply)	masā an-nūr	مساء النور
What is your name?	shū ismak?	شو اسمك
My name is ...	ismī ...	اسمي ...
What is it called in Arabic?	shū ismu bil-‘arabī	شو اسمه بالعربي
How are you (m. sing.)	keif ḥālak	كيف حالك
How are you (f. sing.)	keif ḥālik	كيف حالك
How are you (pl.)	keif ḥālkum	كيف حالكم
Fine, thanks be to God	kwayis, al-ḥamdu-lillāh	كويس الحمد لله
Please (m. sing.)	min fadlak	من فضلك
Please (f. sing.)	min fadlik	من فضلك
Please (pl.)	min fadilkū	من فضلكو

Please, help yourself (m. sing.)		
	itfaddal	اتفضل
Please, help yourself (f. sing.)		
	itfaddalī	اتفضلي
Please, help yourself (pl.)		
	itfaddalū	اتفضلو
Thank you	shukrān	شكراً
You're welcome	'afwān	عفواً
I'm sorry	'āsif/mit'assif	آسف/متأسف
Never mind	basīta (simple)	بسيطة
	ma'lesh (nothing to it)	معليش
Excuse me/beg pardon?		
	'afwān	عفواً
Hopefully, if God wills		
	in shā allah	ان شاء الله
What's wrong with you?		
	esh mālak?	ايش مالك
I'm tired/sick	anā ta'bān	انا تعبان
I'm seriously ill	anā marīd	انا مريض